CONTENTS

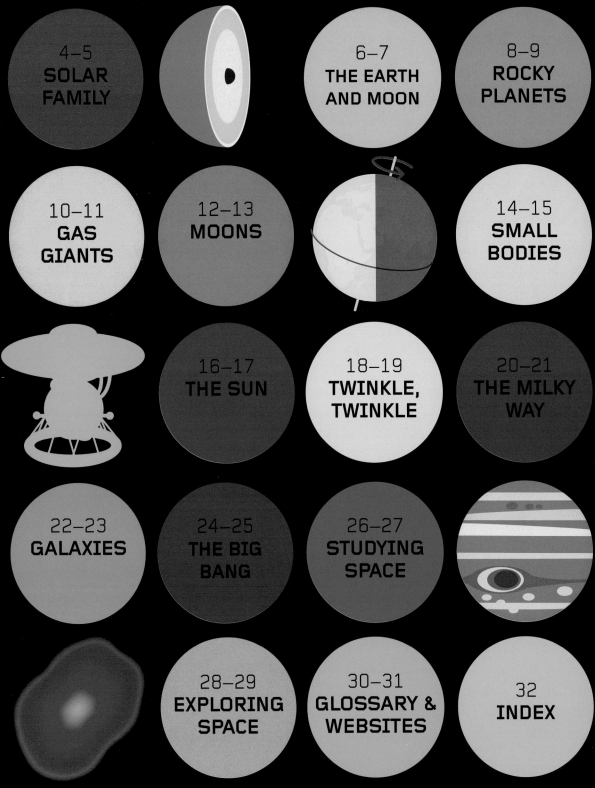

WELCOME TO THE WORLD OF INFOGRAPHICS

Using icons, graphics and pictograms, infographics visualise data and information in a whole new way!

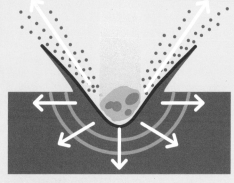

SEE WHAT HAPPENS WHEN AN ASTEROID SLAMS INTO A PLANET

FIND OUT WHAT'S INSIDE THE LARGEST PLANETS IN THE SOLAR SYSTEM

MARVEL AT HOW THE BIGGEST STORM IN THE SOLAR SYSTEM DWARFS PLANET EARTH

COMPARE MOUNT EVEREST TO THE HIGHEST VOLCANO IN THE SOLAR SYSTEM

SOLAR FAMILY

At the centre of the Solar System is a huge ball of burning gas – the Sun. Spinning around this are eight planets, many dwarf planets and millions of small chunks of rock and ice.

0   500   1,000

MARS
EARTH
VENUS
MERCURY
SUN

JUPITER

THE SUN
is our nearest star and it measures 1.4 million kilometres across. It is the largest object in the Solar System, making up more than 99 per cent of the system's mass.

ROCKY PLANETS
The four planets that are nearest to the Sun are mostly made from rocks and metals.

MERCURY   VENUS   EARTH   MARS

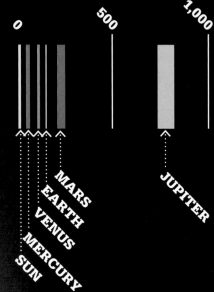

JUPITER

330,000
The Sun has 330,000 times more mass than planet Earth.

ORBITING DISTANCES

The planets go around the Sun in slightly oval-shaped orbits. This means that their distances from the Sun will vary at different points in their orbits.

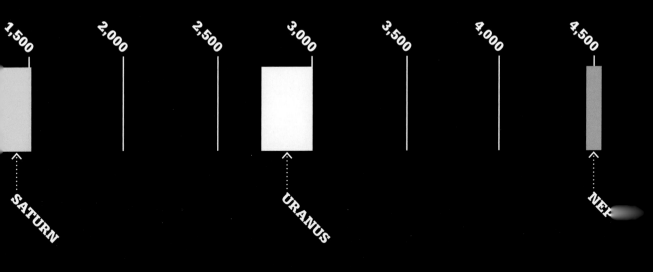

1,500   2,000   2,500   3,000   3,500   4,000   4,500

↑ SATURN   ↑ URANUS   ↑ NEP

GAS GIANTS

The four planets that are farthest from the Sun are enormous balls of gas with solid balls of rocks and metals at their centres.

SATURN

URANUS

NEPTU

8 THE SOLAR SYSTEM HAS EIGHT PLANETS. UP UNTIL 2006, PLUTO WAS COUNTED AS THE NINTH PLANET, BUT IT WAS THEN DOWNGRADED TO A DWARF PLANET

THE EARTH AND MOON

A year is the time it takes for a planet to go around the Sun. During its path around the Sun, the Earth is orbited by the Moon, which goes around the Earth every 27.3 days.

TIDES

The Moon's gravitational pull causes the water of the Earth's oceans to bulge, creating high tides in some areas and low tides in others. As the Earth rotates, the locations of high and low tides change.

23.45°

The angle of the Earth's tilt in relation to the Sun.

SUMMER IN NORTHERN HEMISPHERE

THE EARTH IS FARTHEST FROM THE SUN DURING JULY.

WINTER IN SOUTHERN HEMISPHERE

← · · · · · · · · LOW TIDE

MOON

BULGE OF WATER MARKS HIGH TIDE

AN EARTH YEAR

At two points in its orbit, the Earth has 12 hours of day and 12 hours of night. These are called the equinoxes. The points where the lengths of a day or night are their longest are called the solstices.

← · · · · · · · · LOW TIDE

384,400 KM

Distance from the Earth to the Moon.

30 EARTHS WOULD FIT BACK-TO-BACK IN THE DISTANCE BETWEEN THE EARTH AND THE MOON

NIGHT AND DAY

As the Earth spins around, one half of the planet points towards the Sun and experiences day. At the same time, the other half points away from the Sun and experiences night.

DAY **NIGHT**

Average orbital speed of the Earth around the Sun

107,200 KM/H

SEASONS

At different times of the year, some parts of the planet are tilted towards the Sun, while others are tilted away. The areas tilted towards the Sun experience summer, with long days and warm weather. Those tilted away from the Sun experience winter, with colder weather and shorter days.

SUN

WINTER IN NORTHERN HEMISPHERE

THE EARTH IS CLOSEST TO THE SUN DURING JANUARY

SUMMER IN SOUTHERN HEMISPHERE

EQUATOR

365.3 DAYS

The length of time it takes the Earth to complete one orbit around the Sun.

1 AU

To measure the very large distances around the Solar System, astronomers use astronomical units (AU). One astronomical unit is the distance from the Earth to the Sun, which is approximately

150 MILLION KM.

ROCKY PLANETS

The four planets nearest to the Sun (Mercury, Venus, Earth and Mars) are the smallest in the Solar System. However, these amazing worlds have towering peaks, poisonous atmospheres and surfaces that are both scorching hot and icy cold.

CRUST

UNDER THE SURFACE

The outside of a rocky planet is surrounded by a hard, thin crust. Beneath this, the mantle is usually made from liquid rock. At the centre is a hard core made from metals, such as iron or nickel.

METALLIC CORE

ROCKY MANTLE

ATMOSPHERES

Three of the rocky planets have layers of gases around them called atmospheres. Mercury has an atmosphere, but it is very thin, compared to the other three.

EVEREST EARTH
8,848 M

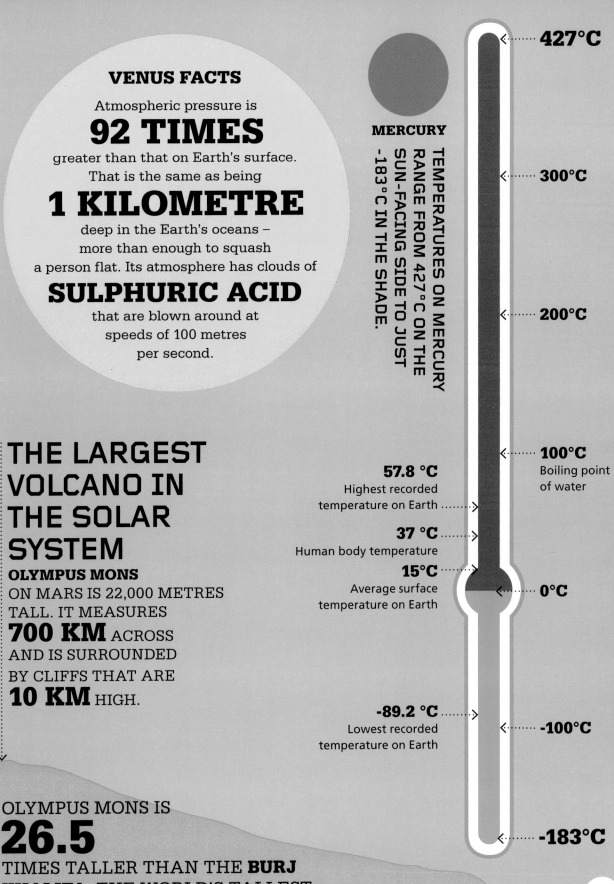

VENUS FACTS

Atmospheric pressure is
92 TIMES
greater than that on Earth's surface.
That is the same as being
1 KILOMETRE
deep in the Earth's oceans –
more than enough to squash
a person flat. Its atmosphere has clouds of
SULPHURIC ACID
that are blown around at
speeds of 100 metres
per second.

MERCURY

TEMPERATURES ON MERCURY RANGE FROM 427°C ON THE SUN-FACING SIDE TO JUST -183°C IN THE SHADE.

THE LARGEST VOLCANO IN THE SOLAR SYSTEM

OLYMPUS MONS
ON MARS IS 22,000 METRES
TALL. IT MEASURES
700 KM ACROSS
AND IS SURROUNDED
BY CLIFFS THAT ARE
10 KM HIGH.

OLYMPUS MONS IS
26.5
TIMES TALLER THAN THE **BURJ KHALIFA**, THE WORLD'S TALLEST BUILDING, WHICH MEASURES 830 M

427°C

300°C

200°C

100°C
Boiling point
of water

57.8 °C
Highest recorded
temperature on Earth

37 °C
Human body temperature

15°C
Average surface
temperature on Earth

0°C

-89.2 °C
Lowest recorded
temperature on Earth

-100°C

-183°C

GAS GIANTS

These gigantic worlds do not have a solid surface. Instead, they are covered with swirling gases that have raging storms and the strongest winds in the Solar System.

OUTER LAYER

INSIDE A GIANT

These gas giants have a very different structure to Earth. Neptune and Uranus have thick layers of gases surrounding a metallic core at the centre. Saturn and Jupiter have outer layers of gases surrounding inner liquid layers and a dense rocky core.

CORE

INNER LAYER

OUTER ATMOSPHERE

The winds on Neptune blow at **2,520 km/h**, making them the fastest winds in the **Solar System.**

GREAT RED SPOT

A powerful storm that's been raging on Jupiter, it is bigger than our planet and has lasted for nearly

350 YEARS

Winds inside the storm reach speeds of up to

432 KM/H

RINGS

All four gas giant planets have systems of rings around their equators. The most visible of these surround Saturn.

URANUS HAS
A TILT OF

98°

URANUS

JUPITER HAS A TILT OF 3.13°

SATURN HAS A TILT
OF 26.73°

NEPTUNE HAS A TILT
OF 28.32°

Saturn's rings stretch for hundreds of thousands of kilometres, but they are only about 10 metres thick. The rings are made up of particles which range in size from specks of dust to

10 METRES

in diameter – bigger than an African elephant.

MOONS

Moons are natural satellites that orbit other bodies. Six of the eight planets in the Solar System have their own moon systems. These moons have frozen seas and explosive volcanoes.

300 KM

COMPARISON OF THE BIGGEST MOONS

GANYMEDE
JUPITER
5,262 KM

TITAN
SATURN
5,152 KM

CALLISTO
JUPITER
4,821 KM

MOON
EARTH
3,476 KM

ICE CRUST

Europa (Jupiter) is covered in an icy surface that may be 30 km thick. In comparison, the ice sheet on Antarctica is just 4.8 km thick.

ICE

CRUST

EUROPA
JUPITER

ICE

CRUST

ANTARCTICA
EARTH

24 KM

VOLCANOES

Volcanoes on the moon Io (Jupiter) throw plumes of material up to 300 km high above the surface. In comparison, the eruption of Mount St Helens in 1980 threw a cloud of ash up to altitudes of just 24 km.

MOON COUNT

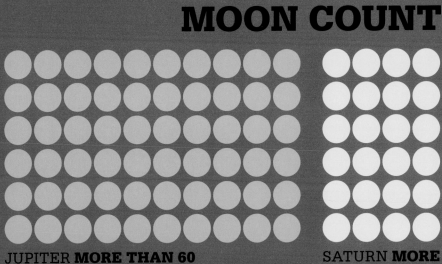

JUPITER **MORE THAN 60**

SATURN **MORE THAN 60**

NEPTUNE **13**

URANUS **27**

MARS **2**   EARTH **1**

SMALL MOONS

Many moons in the Solar System are small and irregularly shaped. Earth's Moon is more than 200 times the width of Mars's tiny moons, Phobos and Deimos.

1610

The year the Italian scientist Galileo Galilei discovered the largest four moons around Jupiter: Callisto, Ganymede, Europa and Io.

DEIMOS
MARS

◄······ **15 KM** ······►

**MANHATTAN,
NEW YORK, USA**

◄ **21.5 KM** ······►

Mars's moon **Phobos** has a declining orbit. This means that it will be **torn apart** by gravity in **10 million** years' time.

SMALL BODIES

As well as the planets, the Solar System contains millions of small bodies. These include dwarf planets, asteroids and comets.

THE ASTEROID BELT

Small pieces of rock that orbit the Sun are called asteroids, or, if they are quite large, they are called dwarf planets. Most of these lie in the Asteroid Belt between Mars and Jupiter.

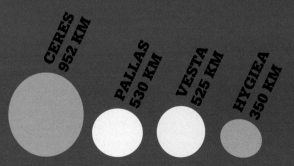

CERES 952 KM

PALLAS 530 KM

VESTA 525 KM

HYGIEA 350 KM

ABOUT HALF THE MASS OF THE BELT IS CONTAINED IN THE FOUR LARGEST ASTEROIDS

952 KM

The diameter of Ceres is 952 km, making it the biggest asteroid in the Asteroid Belt. Ceres is so big that it is called a dwarf planet.

CERES

EARTH 12,756 KM

ASTEROID BELT (NOT TO SCALE)

MARS

JUPITER

COMETS

Comets are lumps of ice, dust and grit that orbit the Sun. A comet's tail will only form as it approaches the Sun.

ORBIT OF COMET

SUN

TAIL

TAIL POINTS AWAY FROM SUN

VENUS

MERCURY

SUN

EARTH

According to **NASA**, there are about **1,290** asteroids that we know of that could **crash into** Earth.

COLLISION!

Sometimes, asteroids and comets slam into planets and moons. When this happens, they create enormous holes in the ground, called craters.

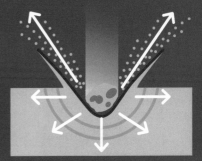

1. Asteroid or comet hits, throwing debris up and out.

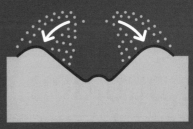

2. The debris settles around the hole creating the lip of the crater.

3. The centre of the hole rises, creating a bulge in the middle.

THE SUN

Our nearest star is the Sun. Far below its surface, tiny atoms are squeezed and squashed until they fuse together. This releases a huge amount of energy, which escapes as light and heat.

PHOTOSPHERE

CONVECTION ZONE

RADIATIVE ZONE

CORE

INSIDE THE SUN

The atomic reactions that create the Sun's heat and light happen deep inside its core. The energy released can take 100,000 years to travel through the upper layers before reaching the surface.

EARTH

,000,000

NUMBER OF TIMES THE EARTH COULD FIT INSIDE THE SUN

SUN

Temperature inside the core

15,000,000°C

SUNSPOTS

These are dark spots that appear on the Sun's surface.

Temperature at the Sun's surface

5,500°C

SOLAR FLARE

This is a massive eruption of burning gas that leaps from the Sun's surface.

SOLAR PARTICLES

The Sun throws out a stream of particles called the solar wind. These particles are deflected towards the Earth's poles by the planet's magnetic field. Here, they react with the atmosphere to create the glowing lights of the aurorae.

NORTH POLE

SOUTH POLE

EARTH'S MAGNETIC FIELD

INCOMING SOLAR PARTICLES

TWINKLE, TWINKLE

Far beyond our Solar System lie trillions of other stars. These stars come in a range of sizes and colours and are often found grouped together in multiple systems or clusters.

MULTIPLES

While the Solar System has only one star, the Sun, many other stars are part of multiple star systems, which contain two or more stars. In fact, most of the stars we can see in the night sky belong to multiple systems.

COLOURS AND SIZES

A star's colour depends on its temperature. Stars that are white and blue are hotter than those that are yellow, orange or red. The largest stars are giants and supergiants, which can be more than 1,000 times bigger than the Sun.

SUN

SIRIUS

POLLUX

ARCTURUS

RIGEL

STAR LIFE AND DEATH

They may look like they shine for ever, but stars are born, live and then die. Depending on how massive they are, they can end their lives as a tiny white dwarf that gradually fades away, or as a powerful black hole, swallowing everything near it.

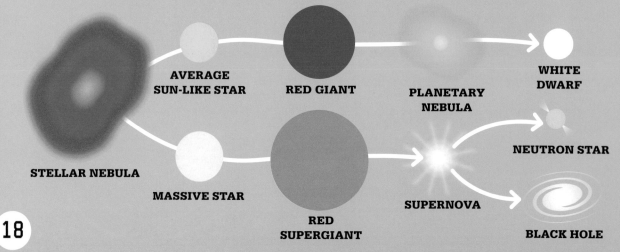

STELLAR NEBULA

AVERAGE SUN-LIKE STAR

RED GIANT

PLANETARY NEBULA

WHITE DWARF

MASSIVE STAR

RED SUPERGIANT

SUPERNOVA

NEUTRON STAR

BLACK HOLE

CONSTELLATIONS

We group the stars we can see in the night sky into pictures and patterns called constellations. Many of these are named after mythical figures, such as Orion the hunter.

88

THE NUMBER OF CONSTELLATIONS INTO WHICH THE NIGHT SKY IS DIVIDED.

ALDEBARAN

BETELGEUSE

SIZE OF THE SWOLLEN SUN

BLACK HOLES

A black hole is an object that is left behind after a massive star dies. Scientists are unsure what black holes are exactly, but they have so much gravity that not even light can escape from them.

SUN ·······>

AT THE END OF ITS LIFE, THE SUN WILL SWELL UP TO FORM A RED GIANT STAR. THIS WILL HAPPEN IN **7,000,000,000** YEARS.

THE MILKY WAY

Stars are grouped together in enormous structures called galaxies. Our galaxy is called the Milky Way and it contains about 200 billion stars.

OUR GALAXY

If you could look down on the Milky Way, it would have a spiral shape, with the stars collected into several arms that orbit around a large centre, called the galactic core. The Milky Way is 100,000 light years across.

50,000 LY

40,000 LY

30,000 LY

20,000 LY

10,000 LY

CARINA-SAGITTARIUS ARM

LIGHT YEARS

Distances in space are so big that astronomers cannot use normal units, such as kilometres. Instead, they use the distance that light can travel in a year. This is called a light year (LY).

PERSEUS ARM

ORION SPUR

OUTER ARM

SUN

SPIRAL ARMS
The Sun and its nearest stars form part of a small arm of the Milky Way called the Orion Spur.

LONG BAR

GALACTIC BAR

CRUX-SCUTUM ARM

GALAXY CENTRE
This measures about 10,000 light years across and is about 6,000 light years thick.

DISTANCE LIGHT WILL TRAVEL IN A NANOSECOND (ONE BILLIONTH OF A SECOND)

30 CM

GALAXIES

The Milky Way is just one of many galaxies that make up the Universe. These enormous objects come in many shapes and sizes and are grouped together in clusters and superclusters.

GALAXY SIZES

While the Milky Way contains some 200 billion stars, our nearest major galaxy, the Andromeda Galaxy, contains up to 400 billion, and is about 200,000 light years in diameter.

200 BILLION

400 BILLION

GALAXY TYPES

ELLIPTICAL

These galaxies range from ball-shaped to oval. They usually have very old stars in them and tend to be much larger than other types of galaxy.

LENTICULAR

Like spiral galaxies, lenticular galaxies have a large central bulge surrounded by a disc. But this disc does not have the curving arms of spiral galaxies.

IRREGULAR

As their name suggests, these galaxies have no clear shape at all.

6,000,000, LY

GALAXY NUMBERS

There are about 170 billion galaxies in the observable Universe (the part of the Universe we can see).

170,000,000,000

BARRED SPIRAL

This is a type of spiral galaxy that has a long bar running through the centre. The size of this bar can vary greatly.

SPIRAL

Spiral galaxies have a large central core that is surrounded by a disc. Stars spiral out along this disc in huge curving arms.

60%

OF ALL KNOWN GALAXIES ARE SPIRAL-SHAPED

COLLIDING

Sometimes, galaxies slam into each other. They will either tear each other apart, or crash together and combine to form a new, larger galaxy.

Many galaxies are found collected together in small groups, which contain up to 50 galaxies, or in clusters, which contain between 50 and several thousand galaxies.

IN TURN, THESE ARE CLUMPED TOGETHER TO FORM SUPERCLUSTERS.

THE SUPERCLUSTER WHICH CONTAINS THE MILKY WAY MEASURES

110 MILLION

LIGHT YEARS ACROSS AND IS MADE UP OF 50,000 GALAXIES.

The Milky Way and Andromeda

galaxies are heading towards each other at

300 km per second and will

collide and merge in about

5,000,000,000

years' time.

THE BIGGEST GALAXIES FOUND MEASURE 6 MILLION LIGHT YEARS ACROSS – THE MILKY WAY IS ONLY ABOUT 100,000 LY.

THE BIG BANG

Scientists can see that all of the distant galaxies are moving away from each other. This indicates that at some time, long ago, everything was much closer together than it is today.

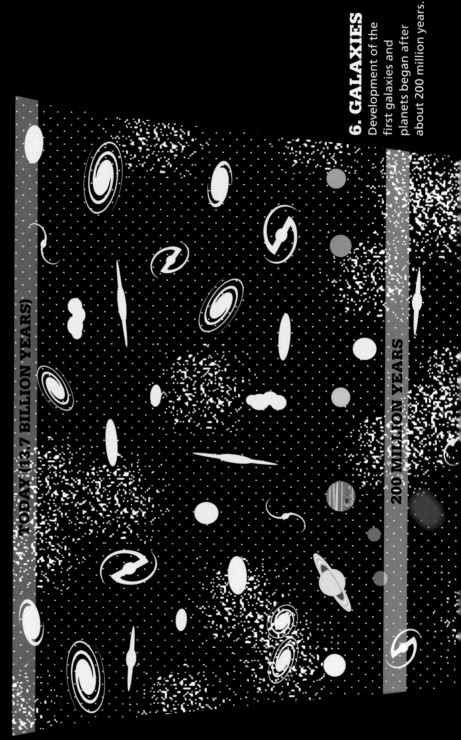

TODAY (13.7 BILLION YEARS)

200 MILLION YEARS

6. GALAXIES

Development of the first galaxies and planets began after about 200 million years.

5. SHINING STARS

The first stars started to shine about 100 million years after the Big Bang.

3. COOLING OFF

After expanding rapidly, space cooled, allowing tiny subatomic particles (electrons, neutrons and protons) to form.

100 MILLION YEARS

500,000 YEARS

3 MINUTES

1 SECOND

1. THE BIG BANG

Scientists believe that the Universe was created in an enormous explosion, which formed all matter. This is also referred to as the Big Bang.

4. ATOMS FORM

Electrons, neutrons and protons combined to form the first atoms about 300,000 years after the Big Bang.

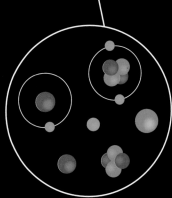

2. INFLATION

In the first few minutes after the Big Bang, the Universe expanded very quickly. During this time, it was like a boiling soup, made up of super-hot particles.

STUDYING SPACE

Astronomers use different telescopes to collect information about the night sky. These telescopes detect the light we can see as well as the energy we cannot, such as infra-red and microwaves, to build up a complete picture of the Universe.

1608 THE YEAR THE FIRST WORKING TELESCOPES WERE MADE.

27
The Very Large Array in New Mexico, USA, is a collection of 27 individual radio dishes that can operate together.

30 M
THE SIZE OF THE MIRROR ON THE NEW TELESCOPE AT MAUNA KEA, HAWAII. IT IS DUE TO BE COMPLETED IN 2018.

305 M
The radio telescope of the Arecibo Observatory in Puerto Rico measures 305 metres across. The enormous dish is set into a natural hollow in a mountain.

RADIO TELESCOPES ARE DISH-SHAPED ANTENNAS. THEY COLLECT THE INVISIBLE RADIO WAVES THAT ARE PRODUCED BY MOST BODIES IN SPACE.

SATELLITES IN ORBIT

Satellites in orbit are in an ideal place to study stars as well as the surface of the Earth. This graphic shows that at a certain height, a satellite will orbit the Earth in the same time it takes the Earth to spin. As such, the satellite stays above the same spot on the Earth's surface. This is called a geostationary orbit.

EQUATOR

ORBIT 35,786 KM ABOVE THE EQUATOR

SPACE TELESCOPES

Space telescopes have a perfect view of the night sky because they are above any distortion caused by the Earth's atmosphere.

THE HUBBLE SPACE TELESCOPE WAS LAUNCHED IN **1990**.
2.4 METRES – THE SIZE OF ITS REFLECTING MIRROR.

HUBBLE

SPITZER

SPITZER

This studies infra-red radiation from star-forming regions and distant planetary systems.

CHANDRA

The Chandra space telescope studies X-rays from very hot parts of the Universe, such as exploded stars and clusters of galaxies.

CHANDRA

RADIO TELESCOPES CAN USE A SINGLE ANTENNA, OR SEVERAL ANTENNAS CAN BE JOINED TOGETHER TO MAKE A BETTER IMAGE.

EXPLORING SPACE

Spacecraft have been blasted to every planet in the Solar System, sending back pictures and rock samples. Humans have even left the Earth and walked on the Moon.

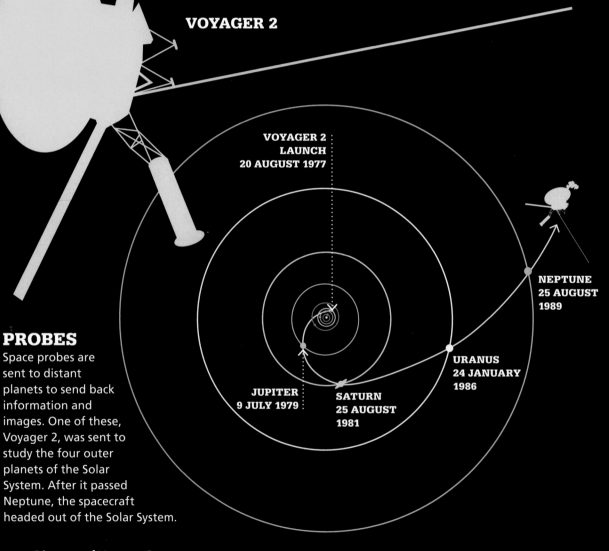

VOYAGER 2

VOYAGER 2
LAUNCH
20 AUGUST 1977

NEPTUNE
25 AUGUST
1989

URANUS
24 JANUARY
1986

JUPITER
9 JULY 1979

SATURN
25 AUGUST
1981

PROBES

Space probes are sent to distant planets to send back information and images. One of these, Voyager 2, was sent to study the four outer planets of the Solar System. After it passed Neptune, the spacecraft headed out of the Solar System.

Distance of Voyager 2 from Earth at the start of 2012

14,600,000,000 KM

1957

Year the first object, Sputnik 1, was sent into space

VENERA 7

landed on Venus in 1970 and became the first man-made spacecraft to touch down on another planet and to transmit data back to Earth.

MAN ON THE MOON

Twelve astronauts landed on the Moon during six Apollo missions. The last person to walk on the Moon was Eugene Cernan during the Apollo 17 mission in 1972.

15 AUG 1971

17 DEC 1972

12 NOV 1969

14 FEB 1971

11 JUL 1969

16 APR 1972

MOON LANDING SITES WITH APOLLO MISSION NUMBER

INTERNATIONAL SPACE STATION

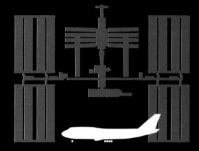

A space station is a spacecraft that can carry a crew and stay in orbit around Earth for a long period of time.

THE INTERNATIONAL SPACE STATION IS ABOUT THE SAME SIZE AS AN AMERICAN FOOTBALL FIELD.

IN ITS FIRST 10 YEARS, IT TRAVELLED ALMOST

2,500,000,000

KILOMETRES IN 57,361 ORBITS AROUND EARTH.

That is the same as eight trips to the Sun and back.

CURIOSITY

Rovers are a type of robot spacecraft that move around a planet's surface. Curiosity is the size of a small car and was designed to explore the surface of Mars, looking for signs of life.

GLOSSARY

atmospheric pressure
The force created by a planet's atmosphere pushing down onto something.

aurorae
Glowing patterns in the sky near to the poles. They are caused by charged particles from the Sun reacting with particles high up in the atmosphere. As well as Earth, aurorae have been spotted on other planets, including Jupiter and Saturn.

Big Bang
The theory that the Universe was formed by an enormous explosion and that all the matter in space was created in the first moments of this event. This matter then joined together to form stars, clouds, galaxies and planets.

star
A large ball of gas whose mass is so great that atoms deep inside its core are squeezed together, fusing them. This releases an enormous amount of energy, which escapes as light and heat.

core
The centre of an astronomical body, such as a planet or a star.

crust
The outer layer of a rocky planet. The crust is usually made up of hard rock.

dwarf planet
A small planet whose body is shaped by its own gravity, but is not big enough to clear its region of other astronomical bodies. Dwarf planets include Pluto, Vesta and Eris, which lie at the very edge of the Solar System.

equinox
A point in the Earth's orbit around the Sun when day and night are equal lengths. There are two equinoxes: in spring and autumn.

galaxy
An enormous collection of stars that are held together by gravity. Galaxies come in many different shapes, including spiral and elliptical.

gravity
The force that attracts one object to another. The amount of gravity an astronomical body has depends on its mass.

orbit
The path of one object around another. For example, the planets of the Solar System follow long, oval-shaped orbits around the Sun, while the Moon orbits the Earth.

An astronomical body that goes around or orbits a star. A planet is big enough to clear its region of other, smaller objects, but is not massive enough to start the fusion of atoms in its core, as happens in the cores of stars. There are eight planets in the Solar System.

The amount of time it takes for a planet to complete one orbit around the Sun. A year on Earth takes about 365 days, and it would complete nearly 12 orbits in the time it takes Jupiter to finish one.

satellite
An astronomical object that orbits another. Moons are natural satellites and they orbit around planets. Artificial satellites are found orbiting Earth where they study space and examine the Earth's surface.

solstice
A point in the Earth's orbit around the Sun when one hemisphere experiences the longest day and shortest night. There are two solstices: one in summer and the other in winter.

tide
The rise and fall of the Earth's oceans caused by the gravitational pull of the Moon and Sun. This pull forms a bulge in the oceans, creating high tide. The tides rise and fall twice each day as the Earth spins around.

moon
A natural satellite in orbit around a larger astronomical body. Moons are found around planets, dwarf planets and even asteroids. The Earth has one moon, while Jupiter has more than 60.

Websites

MORE INFO:
airandspace.si.edu
Website of the Smithsonian Institute's Air and Space Museum. It contains details of exhibitions at the museum as well as teaching resources and online activities.

www.sciencemuseum.org.uk
Homepage of the Science Museum, it features online material, including teacher resources, descriptions of exhibits, games and explanations.

www.nasa.gov/audience/forkids/kidsclub/flash/
The kids page of the NASA website contains fun facts, games, photos and information about space.

MORE GRAPHICS:
www.visualinformation.info
A website that contains a whole host of infographic material on subjects as diverse as natural history, science, sport and computer games.

www.coolinfographics.com
A collection of infographics and data visualisations from other online resources, magazines and newspapers

www.dailyinfographic.com
A comprehensive collection of infographics on an enormous range of topics that is updated every single day!

INDEX

ACKNOWLEDGEMENTS

Published in 2013 by Wayland
Copyright © Wayland 2013

Wayland
338 Euston Road
London NW1 3BH

Wayland Australia
Level 17/207 Kent Street
Sydney NSW 2000

All rights reserved.
Senior editor: Julia Adams
Produced by Tall Tree Ltd
Editor: Jon Richards

Designer: Ed Simkins
Consultant: Professor Raman Prinja

British Library Cataloguing in Publication Data
Richards, Jon, 1970-
  The world in infographics.
  Space.
  1. Outer space--Pictorial works--Juvenile
  literature.
  I. Title II. Space III. Simkins, Ed.
  523.1-dc23

ISBN: 9780750278454
10 9 8 7 6 5 4 3 2 1
Printed in China

Wayland is a division of Hachette
Children's Books, an Hachette UK company.
www.hachette.co.uk

The website addresses (URLs) included in this
book were valid at the time of going to press.
However, because of the nature of the Internet,
it is possible that some addresses may have
changed, or sites may have changed or closed
down, since publication. While the author and
Publisher regret any inconvenience this may
cause the readers, no responsibility for any such
changes can be accepted by either the author
or the Publisher.